Sun... & Semicolons

FROM CREATIVITY
TO MECHANICS
TO PUBLISHING

**A FRANK & REVEALING FIELD GUIDE
TO THE WRITER'S LIFE**

Writing down the Bones
Natalie Goldberg

GREG LILLY

Cherokee McGhee

Williamsburg, Virginia

ISBN 978-1-937556-03-7

First Edition 2013

Cover design by Braxton McGhee

Published by:
Cherokee McGhee, L.L.C.
Williamsburg, Virginia

Find us on the World Wide Web at:
WWW.CHEROKEEMCGHEE.COM

Printed in the United States of America

Sunsets

&

Semicolons

Jenny—
Thanks for the
support!
Greg Lilly

GREG LILLY

Sunsets

&

Semicolons

Contents

The Real Writing Life

"You are really living the dream," a fellow writer said to me. My first response was *What the heck? This is the writing dream?*

But then as I thought about it, I make my living by writing. I admit it's not a living of tropical island hideaways and using jet as a verb, but I can pay my bills while doing something I love.

If that is your goal, I can give you some advice on the rocky trail to this place. It ain't easy. You have to love writing to stay with it. Honestly, flipping hamburgers is less stressful and gives you a steady paycheck. But, you don't get people e-mailing you or stopping by a book signing table to say how much they enjoyed a story you created — a story born from your own imagination. That's pretty cool.

How I ended up here...

In high school, I didn't care for my English classes. That could have been because of the strict requirements to focus on certain things like grammar, vocabulary, sentence diagrams, Shakespeare, or analysis. I was a math and science geek.

In college, I enjoyed the literature classes and used most of my electives in Virginia Tech's Department of English. With an information technology degree from Tech, my first job was to write technical manuals, train employees on computer systems, and eventually program computer-based training (today's on-line learning).

My documentation developed plots and characters, which management didn't enjoy. The vice-president of technology suggested I try fiction writing on the weekends. I found a group of other like-minded corporate workers, and we formed a critique group that meet twice a month for wine and writing. This is where I developed the basic craft of writing — over a period of many years (and I'm still developing it all these years later).

Twenty years of corporate technology, project management, technical training, documentation and staff meetings led to an itch to take off across the country for adventure.

Go west young man... And reinvent yourself

My partner and I, the cat and the Great Dane, we sold all we could and relocated to the amazing "New West" of Sedona, Arizona. Enlightenment, awe-inspiring skies, red rocks, and artists surrounded us, but brought a whack of reality to the dream.

The high-paying, professional jobs of corporate America didn't exist in the tourist-driven town. I used my fiction writing samples and my project management experience to land a managing editor job at a regional magazine focused on the high desert homes and gardens.

From there I moved to an art gallery to write artist biographies, press releases on art shows, create ads for glossy art magazines, and other operational duties.

I published my first two novels with a small independent publisher. I learned to promote and sell the books around Sedona and on the Internet.

Go east young man... And reinvent yourself again

Aging parents and family commitments beckoned us back to the East Coast. Timing was bad with the Great Recession slapping every job seeker in the gut.

I decided to go freelance, write for my living. I found a few jobs that allowed me time to build my publishing company. The magazine job had taught me how to publish a magazine. The ad creating at the art gallery taught me how to create layouts and how to promote. My technology background gave me the confidence to jump on the computer and teach myself all the software needed to produce a novel. I used my finished manuscript *Under a Copper Moon* to test my procedures and strategies. With the money it made, I published another author's work, and then another and another.

I knew I couldn't make a living on just the royalties from my own books because I couldn't write them fast enough. I needed to bring together a group of authors that I felt needed to be read, to be promoted, to be published. I had the skills and knowledge to do that. The Cherokee McGhee publishing house was born.

Be flexible and innovative

For those of us who have not retired, we need to have multiple sources of income. One book's royalties will not do that, unless you are J.K. Rowling or Stephenie Meyer (and they have produced multiple books before the first ones took off).

Look at your skills and experience. I used my computer skills and marketing knowledge to get some jobs, and then my project management experience to land others. When there were no jobs to be found, I created my own.

I teach writing and publishing workshops. That came to me because I missed conducting the classes I had taught on technology. Workshops are fun for me because I enjoy time with other writers. Days get long when you spend ten to twelve hours in front of a computer screen.

Sunsets & Semicolons

This book came from those workshops I teach. I love handouts. For the workshops, I found that I had stacks of handouts for each session. This is a collection of my writing workshops. I'm sure I'll revise it from time to time with more discoveries and suggestions.

For now, this is one writer's life, from creativity to craft, from staring at sunsets to sweating over semicolons. This is my opinion, but certainly not the only one out there. These tips and suggestions have worked for me over time, and I hope they give you some guidance and a few sparks of insight.

The following chapters are from my 25 years of reading every writing book and article I could find, attending workshops, trying new and old methods, then adapting and molding the information to what worked for me. I mention books that I found particularly helpful.

Writing is a verb. You do it. It keeps going. You never finish learning and growing.

This guide does not teach you how to write. It gives you tips for the trenches of writing: developing an idea so it makes it to the page; overcoming writer's block when the words don't flow; strengthening the pace of the manuscript so readers are breathless; and finally, how to sell your manuscript to a publisher — from an insider's viewpoint.

Test that Idea

On average, every third book signing I hold, someone will come up and say: *I have a great idea for a book.* I smile and try to sell them a book that I have already written instead of committing to take on their project, which is what they are trying to initiate.

Ideas for great books fly through the air like dragonflies on a humid August afternoon. Catching one and developing it into a compelling story is where the sweating starts.

Most people don't want to sweat. They would rather be the "idea person" and have a writer execute it for them. This is the celebrity method of authorship. If you are not Jennifer Lopez, Oprah Winfrey, or James Patterson, you will have to write your own book. Okay, that last example was snarky. I'm sure James Patterson writes all his books.

A short story, a novella, a screenplay, or a novel takes a lot of effort. I know writers with burning ideas, concepts that haunt them for years, but when they sit down to capture it on paper, to expand it into plot and characters, the idea fizzles on the page.

What the heck happened?

Check the Plot's Wings

First, write down the idea

Explore the idea a bit to see if you can put into words why it's buzzing around your head.

As an example, I'll use an idea I had for a short story that never got past the first draft. If this develops, I might work on it again.

Idea Worksheet

1	What is the idea for the story?
2	What ignited this idea for you?
3	What keeps it burning in your mind?

My example:

1	What is the idea for the story?
	A world without religion

2	What ignited this idea for you?
	The wars and violence caused by fervent religious ideological beliefs
3	What keeps it burning in your mind?
	News stories from around the world and Ray Bradbury's what-if short stories

Do you have a story?

The simplest form for a story is:

> (**Character**) wants (**goal**) because (**motivation**), but faces (**conflict**).

That means a story needs:

- a character

- a goal

- a motivation

- a conflict

Think of these as your basic mechanisms to get off the ground.

Now, I'll try to apply some specifics to this idea that could turn it into a story. I use a *Story Worksheet* to record those story elements.

Story Worksheet

1	What is the main character's name?
2	What does he/she want to achieve?
3	Why does the character want this?
4	What keeps the character from reaching this goal?

My Example:

1	What is the main character's name?
	James
2	**What does he/she want to achieve?**
	Unite his "tribe" of friends and family to a higher sense of purpose
3	**Why does the character want this?**
	His friends and family seem to be self-centered, narcissistic and disengaged
4	**What keeps the character from reaching this goal?**
	Apathy of the people and rule of science

Now, I have a character James wanting to rally his friends to get them to care about things other than themselves, but their apathy and life based on science and logic stand in his way.

Prepare for Takeoff

Once you have the *Story Worksheet*, there are several techniques to stretch those wings and get some energy flowing. You may find your own way of adding some details, or you may try one of these that has helped me:

A Loose Outline

I'm not a big outliner, but when I first get an idea, I like to get some structure recorded.

> This can be as simple as the high points of the main plot and a few ideas for sub plots.
>
> > - Show James dealing with the self-centeredness of the people around him
> > - Some incident that results in a death because people lacked concern for others
> > - James studies old books that talk of religion
> > - He realizes that religion created a community
> > - He begins to rally people to the idea of something more important than themselves
> > - He becomes a prophet
> > - People focus on his words
> > - An Us vs. Them mentality develops
> > - A neighboring community is seen as a threat
> > - etc...
>
> You can see it isn't a formal outline. The points aren't of equal strength or significance, but are steps in the story.

A Candy Land™ Map

This is as fun as it sounds. Think of that Hasbro Candy Land™ board game that we all played as children.

The game board didn't have a lot of words to read, but pictures that went along a path. We're writers, so we'll use a few more words instead of pictures along our path.

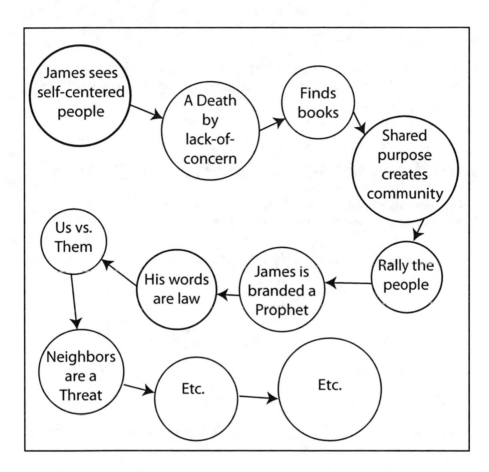

Creating a map of how you think the story should flow is a great visual. I tend to be a visual person, so I really like this method of fleshing out a story.

You can use circles like the illustration above or any graphic that works for you.

I have written ideas on index cards and arranged them on the floor. "Sticky notes" work on the wall or door, if you want to be vertically-oriented.

Have fun with it.

Soar or Crash?

You may run out of steam after a few steps. That's fine. Better to know at this point than to force something that doesn't excite your imagination.

Another Method — Character-Driven

If that crashed, don't despair. Maybe it was the wrong *goal* for that *character*. Consider the story form again:

> (**Character**) wants (**goal**) because (**motivation**), but faces (**conflict**).

Stories usually fall into two broad categories:

- plot-driven
- character-driven

When I get in a hurry, I tend to pick the wrong goal for a character or the wrong character for a particular goal.

First...

decided which idea excites you the most: the character or the plot?

Then...

expand on that to discover a more intriguing relationship between character and plot.

Here is a checklist of things to consider.

- ☐ Who is the most logical character to be the hero of this plot?

- ☐ Who would be a surprise hero for this plot?

- ☐ Which character has the most to overcome to be a hero?

- ☐ How does this plot test the mettle of each character?

- ☐ Do you know your characters well enough to understand how they could react to a situation? No? Let's do a quick Character Study to help you get to know them better:

  Ask yourself 20 questions about this character:

  1. What is her full name?

  2. What is her nickname?

  3. How does she dress?

  4. What are her outstanding physical features?

  5. Where is her favorite place? Why?

  6. What is she afraid of? Why?

  7. Where does she live? Why?

  8. Who does she live with? Why?

  9. What is her biggest secret?

  10. What is her biggest problem?

  11. Does she have a family? Who are they?

  12. What does she love?

  13. What does she hate?

  14. What does she collect/what objects draw her attention?

  15. What's her pet peeve?

  16. What's her biggest flaw?

17. What's her secret wish?

18. What's one more unique thing about this character?

19. Who is her enemy? Why?

20. How far would she go to reach her goal?

This checklist will help you know your character better.

Excited yet? You should have a better understanding if your idea is character-driven or plot-driven.

Let's go back to the story form again:

(**Character**) wants (**goal**) because (**motivation**), but faces (**conflict**).

WIth this enhanced understanding of your character and plot, try the *Story Worksheet* (on page 8) again. You will bring new energy to the idea.

This can be a cyclical process. Try changing different elements of the story to discover which combination creates an exciting project.

Still No Energy?

When you cannot get an idea to take flight, just ground it and move on. Do not force the idea because the resulting piece will hold little enjoyment for you. The writing will become work.

This is supposed to be fun. Hold out for that stimulating idea that makes you want to write deep into the night. Your story will soar!

Overcoming Writer's Block

Many writers don't write. They revise and revise and revise one chapter until it is perfect. But, guess what? It will never be perfect.

This constipated process of editing is a way to avoid writing. When a writer avoids writing, he avoids criticism of his writing. He avoids moving on to another idea. He avoids finishing.

A writer who doesn't write is keeping the embryonic idea from growing and taking on its own life. Constant revision of the first few chapters of a novel is like nursing a newborn for years — like for 20 years — and not letting it mature.

Okay, that's all the bodily function metaphors I can use for this. Just blow it out, you can clean it up later.

This chapter explores ways to get words on the page.

Whether you are working on a memoir, short story, novel, non-fiction book, article, personal journal or a poem, the process can be stalled before completion. Don't let that happen.

Writer's Block — What Is It?

It is avoidance, fear, pride, over-thinking...

There could be a lot of psychological aspects to writer's block, but it comes down to simply not getting words on the page.

Doesn't matter if it's good writing or not. Write it down.

Simple?

Nope. There is a mental hurdle that has to be jumped to prove that you can do it again and again. The following techniques have worked for me.

Techniques for Finishing

Getting started is hard, but finishing is a rare accomplishment.

What are the barriers to finishing a project? Or even getting started on one?

- Ideas / inspiration / creativity
- Time
- Doubt / fear

We'll tackle each one of these with techniques that have worked for me and other writers I know.

Uncovering Ideas

No ideas? No inspiration? No creativity? Nonsense.

Here are several ways to break through those walls.

Automatic Writing

I have always found Natalie Goldberg's "automatic writing" a real declogger of ideas.

Add this to your To-Read list:
"Writing Down the Bones" by Natalie Goldberg

The automatic writing technique has been around in different forms for years.

Basically, just keep the pen moving for a set amount of time, for example 15 minutes.

Start with a prompt, such as:

- Describe the quality of light coming through the window

- I remember when…

- Take a line of poetry, then write it down. Use it as a jumping off point. When you run out of steam, write it down again and go.

EXERCISE:

I remember when I first saw the beach or waded through a mountain creek…

Now write for 15 minutes. Don't stop moving the pen. If you run out of things to write, just rewrite the prompt and go.

15 minutes later…

What was the dominant theme in your writing – the nugget that you focused on? This could be an idea for an article or story.

Passions

Write about something you are passionate about (or at least really interested in).

EXERCISE:
>   Make a list of those passions. For example:
>
>   - landscaping
>
>   - turkey vultures
>
>   - motorcycles
>
>   - the dignity of your grandmother
>
>   - what really happens behind the doors of a gated-community
>
>   - early 20th century history — the Roaring 20s
>
>   - deer hunting
>
>   - long-lost friendships
>
>   - genealogy

What do you read?

Many times passions are revealed when you review your bookcase to look for a common theme.

EXERCISE:
>   Make a list of topics that interest you…(some categories to help you get started). For example:
>
>   - Environmental
>
>   - Political
>
>   - Relationships

- Financial

- Health

- Historical

- New Age

- Mystery

- Thrillers

Stalled Writing

When you just feel like you have run out ideas of what to write next, here are a few techniques that work.

- Brainstorming — what we just did in the exercises above. Make a list of things that could happen or list conflicts between characters.

- Bubble graph – structured brainstorming. This is one of my favorite techniques.

  I use the "bubble graph" when I get stuck in plotting a story. This is basically a brainstorming tool adapted from my days in Information Technology and Project Management.

1. Start by drawing a circle (on paper, on a whiteboard, on your wall) and write the current character situation in that circle.

2. Next think about what could happen next. What's the best thing? What's the worst? What if a friend showed up? An enemy? What if the phone rang? What if the TV broadcast a tornado warning? What if a car screeched to a stop outside the house? This is your time to play What If.

3. Each scenario creates a circle off that middle circle and you have a new situation (a story turn) to think about. Repeat the process until you have a series of linked bubbles.

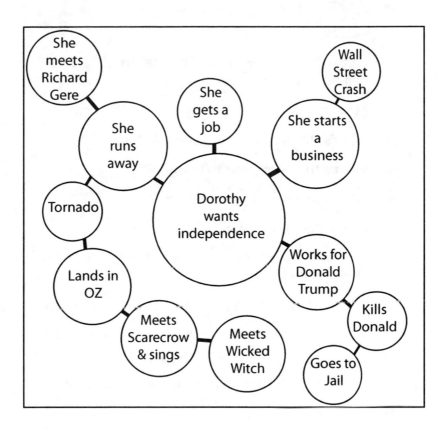

4. Review the paths created by your ideas. Some will not go very far – they hit a wall. Others will continue spurring new ideas and greater possibilities for the plot. These are the storylines that inspire and excite you.

I use this for many things: overcoming writer's block, pushing a story forward, reviewing plots and subplots after the first draft, and even in non-fiction to help construct the flow of an article.

When you feel like you're at a dead end, start drawing bubbles and discover your possibilities.

- What if…

  Like the branches off the Bubble Graph, a What if question can prompt new ideas.

  Make a simple list that begins with What if…

- What's the worst thing that could happen?

- What's the best thing to happen?

- Why is this person doing this?

  Motivation – get multiple answers

  When I wrote *Under a Copper Moon*, I used this technique and started with:

  Why does Inez move across country to a mining town?

  - She sees adventure in the newspaper ad
  - She has no prospects at home
  - Lottie's attitude makes her question society's rules

EXERCISE:

  Explore your character's motivations. Make a list of questions to get to the real reasons.

  For example, a character who is running for elected office. Some questions you could ask yourself about her motivations are:

  - Why does she want to be in office?
  - Really?
  - What's in it for her?

Writing Memoirs? Motivation and results are always

important. Think of it as a "lessons learned" piece. Always ask "Why?" What did I learn from that experience that made me who I am?

- Scene stalled: See the action...Play the scene in your mind; act it out – step by step.

Step away from your desk and computer. Become the character. Act out the fight scene or love scene or cake baking scene. Use your spouse or neighbor if you need others to act with.

Especially for high-action scenes, slow down the movements so that you can describe each one. Write it out in detail. You can always edit it if the actions run too long.

- Read – research a topic; reading will spark connections/ ideas.

I have found that historical fiction is as much about the culture of the time as the actual storyline.

When I wrote *Under a Copper Moon*, I read all I could about the history of the town, copper mining, the late Victorian/ early Edwardian eras in the western United States, and the status of women during the time.

Researching unveils subplots that can be woven into the story.

Getting on Track

Ever feel you have taken a tangent from the story? You look around at what you've written and nothing seems familiar.

How the heck did I get here?

Maybe you did the Bubble Graph and took a branch that was exciting but not consistent to where you wanted to go. Time to reevaluate the road you have taken.

- **What is this story about?**

  Revisit the idea you had for the story. Here are some techniques to get back on track:

  - Focus on the theme

    What is the theme you are conveying with the story? Does the current scene support that? How can it?

    Sometimes, I find the characters acting out on a situation or having a conversation that I find interesting, but has nothing to do with the theme of the story. Usually it can be tweaked to support the story line. If not, kill it, delete it, stomp on it...or set it aside as an idea for a future story.

  - *TV Guide* method

    When I was growing up, we always had a *TV Guide* next to the television. Before remote controls that allowed channel surfing or on-screen guides, we used a paper-based magazine that told us what shows were scheduled on each station.

    The guide listed a description of each show or movie, usually limited to one sentence. Yes, only one sentence.

    Describe your story in one sentence.

    > "The police chief of a New England vacation community, although terrified of the ocean, sets out to destroy a huge killer shark" – *Jaws* by Peter Benchley

    > "A group of British schoolboys, attempting to survive after their plane crashes on a tropical island, begin reverting to savagery." – *Lord of the Flies* by William Golding

This technique reminds you of your basic plot and helps to ensure that each chapter, each scene, each sentence moves the reader in the right direction. This sentence can be posted next to your computer.

- Revisit your tone & approach

Are you spending too much time on the love subplot of your horror story? Is your hero saved by the comic relief character? Has the tone of your children's story turned dark? Is your middle grade adventure focused on existentialism?

Take a look at your approach to the theme and plot. Is this path the best way for you to illustrate what you want to say?

Is the tone distracting to the plot? Or maybe you have come across an innovative approach. Remember: When Bram Stroker wrote *Dracula*, he never intended for his monster, a vampire, to be sexy. Now, you can't find one that doesn't look like a super model or act like a wounded puppy.

- To outline or not to outline?

There are two camps in the discussion of outlines: those who do and those who don't. Okay, maybe three camps with the third being a hybrid outline.

Outlines with Roman numerals, letters — both capitalized, and later, lower case, along with numbers have haunted writers since elementary school. Some writers swear by them. We call them the "Outliners." Other writers prefer to go it alone with just their creativity leading the way. We call them the "Seat-of-the-Pantsers."

For non-fiction, an outline is usually required for the structure it forces. Chapters in non-fiction books usually have a progression that takes the readers from one point to the next, building on each idea.

For fiction, I was a total Pantser through my first four novels. I found it difficult to map out chapters and scenes while still feeling creative. Sometimes I would outline after the first draft to review the structure of the plot I had created.

SUGGESTION: *Don't be strict about outlines.*

> I have found that while going by the seat-of-my-pants, I might get stuck as to where to go next. I tried an outline. It worked.

> Outline what you have done so far. That should help you see the direction and what still needs to happen. It will reveal the next steps for your plot.

- Hybrid outlining

Another useful outlining technique for fiction writers is the hybrid version. Throw the Roman numerals and letters — both capital and lower case — to the wind. List where you want to start the story and where you want to end. Then fill in with major events or scenes you think you will need in between to arrive at that ending. Just use enough detail to remind you of what you should be writing toward.

This leaves plenty of space for the Pantsers to be creative and gives some structure to make sure you arrive on time and under budget.

- Graph the story arc

Another technique for "Getting on Track" is a visual perspective of the story arc. The story arc is structure of the plot's high and low points, action and contemplation, tension and release.

Writers subscribe to different types of story arcs, each writer enjoying a favorite that seems to work for him/her.

I tend to change mine to fit the story, but I like to graph the action so I can visually assess the structure.

You may hear about five-act, three-act, eight-point, and so on, but I suggest doing what feels right for your particular story. I have spent many dead end paths trying to impose a certain structure, only to throw it all out and do what feels right. But, I come back and graph the arc just to double check that I'm not jerking the reader with too many conflicts and not enough recovery periods.

A graphed story arc might look like this:

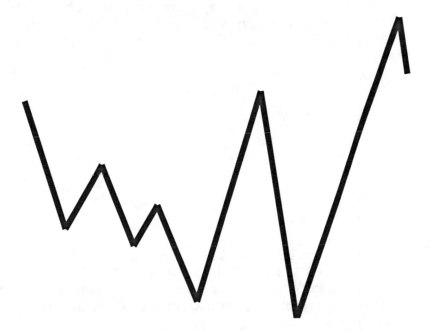

This shows how the story starts off fast, but then goes through peaks and valleys. This keeps the reader's interest as the character struggles toward his goal. About two-thirds through the story, the character almost achieves his goal, but the villain wages a final battle that knocks the hero down and he has to summon all his wits to win.

- Narrow your scope

If you feel off track, is it because you are taking on something too large? Are you trying to tell the tale of a family through several generations? Are you overwhelmed by the task?

Put it down in writing, so you can see the scope of your

project:

1	What is the time frame covered in the plot?
2	Who are the major characters? (Characters who will develop and change over the course of the story.)
3	What are the subplots that intertwine around the main plot? (The more subplots you have the more complex the story and the longer the story.)

4	Overwhelmed?
	Try reducing the time frame covered by the story, combine characters where possible so you have maybe two or three major characters and several minor ones. and/or simplifying your plot and subplots.

SUGGESTION: *Think of plot lines like braiding a girl's hair.*

Three work well for crossing over and creating a nice tight braid. Think of the strands as the main plot and two subplots weaving together. This is the minimum number of plot lines for a novel.

If you have a plot and want to add subplots, add at least two. You can't create a braid with anything less.

- Know your audience

Still feeling off track? Think about who you are writing for. Who will read this story?

When I wrote technical manuals, this was the main focus on keeping the subject on track. A person who is going to use a computer program to write a purchase order, doesn't care how the computer processes the data in bits and bytes.

Keep focused on the reader.

What is the story about and why does a reader care?

A young adult novel might personalize cultural conflicts in the meeting of two characters, but the history and founding of those cultures would be more than a reader can endure.

Finding the Time

One of the biggest complaints about Writer's Block is that there just isn't enough time in the day to get my "butt in the chair" and write. Below are several ways that have worked for me in carving out writing time when I'm working a 40-50 hour a week full-time job.

- Morning Pages

  One of my favorite books on creativity is Julia Cameron's *The Artist's Way.* The book is a twelve week workshop on recovering your creativity. I've gone through the workshop several times with different groups of people and always had a tremendous awakening in my creativity. I recommend it to everyone.

  One of the tasks that Julia Cameron assigns during the workshop duration (and afterwards as well) is what she labels "Morning Pages."

  This is also one of the things that participants in the program fight. She asks that each person write three pages, continuous writing, no thinking, no stopping until you have filled three pages in your notebook.

  The part that people rally against is that she says to do this first thing in the morning, as soon as you wake. No coffee first, no brushing of your teeth, no breakfast or newspaper — just get up and start writing stream-of-consciousness until three pages are covered with your scrawlings.

  The reason people (and I) found this so difficult was that Julia Cameron wanted us to change our morning rituals. She pushed writing into our routine. Each of us has certain things we do within the first 30 to 60 minutes of waking up, and we always do that, every morning.

  My morning routine: wake, go to the bathroom, head to the kitchen to start coffee, take vitamins with orange juice, turn on the television morning news, retrieve the newspaper from the driveway, pour coffee in the same cup, glance at the paper, sit down in front of the television and watch the local news.

Yep, it's boring and predictable, but it is what I like to do to glide into the day. Now, here comes Ms. Julia Cameron, who I have only met once, and she wants me to change that routine? Bitch, please. (Just kidding, she's a very nice woman.)

The brilliant part of the Morning Pages task is that it is in the morning. The morning is a time that we all have a routine and if we can wedge something in, it will likely stay.

- Find your own time

If mornings work for you, great. Get up an hour earlier while the house is quiet and everyone else is still asleep. Or work it into your daily morning ritual — skip the morning TV news or the newspaper and use that time to write.

Finding time for my first novel *Fingering the Family Jewels — a Derek Mason Mystery,* I used my lunch hour at work. I would go to the cafeteria and get a sandwich to bring back to my cubicle and write while I ate. That was an hour each day of drafting the book. I used time on the weekend to edit what I had written during the workweek.

When I lived in Sedona, Arizona, I would get up at 5:00 a.m. (not bad because during the summer the sun was starting to come up then — Arizona doesn't subscribe to Daylight Saving Time). I would take my morning run around the neighborhood in the breaking dawn then go into my home office for an hour before I needed to get ready for work. I wrote my novel *Under a Copper Moon* on that schedule.

- Claim your own time

Communicate to everyone in the household that you are **working** during that time. You will not accept any interruptions. This is why the early morning works well while spouses, children, and pets are still sleeping.

- Stake your ground

  Find a place of your own that you can write. This helps other people see that you are physically in another area and that it is writing time. This doesn't have to be anything fancy, but it should be a place where you can close the door or remove yourself from the regular traffic patterns of the family.

  A study or home office with a door that can be closed is perfect. The bathroom works too. No one will bother you in the bathroom — if you have another one that the family can use while you're holed up writing.

  No peace at home? Head out to a coffee shop, the library, or a park bench.

- Deadline yourself

  I love critique groups for the simple reason of giving myself a deadline. I was part of a critique group in Charlotte, North Carolina from 1988 through 2003. We met every two weeks. If I showed up for more than two or three meetings without something to read, the other writers would ask why I wasn't writing. That buddy system of writing to share with others helps me. It may help you too.

  Beside the deadline of meeting with a group of other writers, an effective method is setting a deadline for yourself. To make this work, you should tell other people about your deadline so you feel responsible for hitting it.

  For *Under a Copper Moon*, I set the deadline of finishing the first draft by the end of the year. The story had been lingering. I loved the characters I had created. I liked spending time with them. This was in September and I made the resolution to have the draft finished by the end of the year. I wanted the new year to start with me doing revisions on the book. I told everyone that I would be finished by December 31.

- Drop the guilt

Forget the guilt of not sticking to your daily schedule, things happen.

If you find yourself avoiding the writing time, that's okay because maybe you just need a break. Go for a walk instead and think about the story, the characters, and the plot lines.

Is the story progressing in a way that has lost your enthusiasm?

Whip out the Bubble Graph and see if there is another branch that excites you more. Take the story in that direction. You are the author; it's your world; kill off the boring character; let the good girl act bad; spice it up.

Remember that you can always rewrite later. Play with the story. Have fun.

Just write.

It's okay to take a break. Writing shouldn't feel like labor. There's enough of that without imposing it on yourself.

Doubting Thomas

Even Jesus had a critic in the Apostle Thomas. Writers have critics too, before the words hit the page. Your internal editor can be nasty and brutal.

Each of us has the proverbial devil and angel watching over our actions.

A writer's angel is the artist creating stories and writing beautiful, free-flowing words that express emotion and insight into the human condition. Her reward is the stream of words on the page.

The writer's devil is that bitchy, crabby critic who says the writing stinks, who suggests the plot is trite, who refuses creativity, who sneers at the play of words. HIs reward is for the writer to stop writing.

Squelching the critic is difficult. We are taught to be modest and to think we're not creative.

Try to write without judgement. This is hard, but remind yourself that there will be time to go back and edit later.

Get the words on the page first. Lock up the critic until it is time to revise.

Anne Lamott calls these critic-free writings "shitty first drafts" in her book *Bird by Bird*. Buy this book and read it if you are having trouble keeping the critic at bay.

Give yourself permission to get the story on paper. No one will see it but you. You can always go back later and change it or even delete it.

Like I said earlier, I would write during my lunch hour or in the mornings, and then use the weekends to edit and revise. The angel artist flew with me during the week. The devil critic was let out of his cage on the weekend to corral the wild prose and over-the-top imagery. This helped me ensure I was on track and ready for another week of creating.

The critic isn't all bad. In fact, he's necessary when it is time for him.

Take Criticism in Stride

Along with that internal critic who tries to stop you from writing, there are the external critics.

One of the most difficult things for a writer to do, besides writing, is separating themselves from criticism.

Whether criticism comes from your critique group, your spouse, or after the book is published, an amateur or professional critic, the comments are on the execution of the writing and ideas, not of you as a person. Remember, it is only an opinion influenced by that person's state of mind at the time.

A phrase that I keep with me from Julia Cameron's books is that harsh critics are really nothing more than "blocked creatives." This makes sense to me because people who are happily creative and producing work are encouraging to all others because they know how freeing creativity is and how difficult it is to let creativity flow.

The critics I value are the ones who offer constructive criticism, ways to make the work better. Discard anything that feels like a personal attack — those statements are about the critic, not about you or your work.

SUGGESTION: *Take what works and discard the rest.*

My friend and fellow writer Michelle Moore (author of *Jasper*) always says to take critique group suggestions that ring true to you and pass over the rest. Only you, the author, knows the right direction and execution of the manuscript. The manuscript is **your** work, not a group work.

Let 'er Flow

When you feel stalled, rundown, slapped around, take a deep breath and try one of these techniques to get the writing flowing again.

You can finish your manuscript. It will be a manuscript with more creativity, focus, and the most important ingredient — a satisfied author.

Books I love on overcoming writer's block:

- *The Artist's Way* by Julia Cameron

- *Writing Down the Bones* by Natalie Goldberg

- *Bird by Bird* by Anne Lamott

Pick Up The Pace

What is Pace?

Pace is keeping the story moving. Think of it as one step after another that is charged with action and emotion.

Pace is the rhythm of your writing. From the overall story to the chapter, scene, paragraph, and sentence, each element of the manuscript contributes to the pace.

Break-neck, jogging, contemplative... It's all pace.

Two main components in writing: Show & Tell

Show is the action (Fast)

Tell is the explanation (Slow)

Participants in my workshops always ask how they will know when to show and when to tell... the answer is: *It depends.*

Experience helps decide when to speed up and slow down –- like running (sprint versus jog).

Some pace decisions will come naturally. Exciting parts of the story inherently speed up, while there must be some "recover" time.

The overall story arc is to start with action then "heartbeat" down and up, building to the climax of the story.

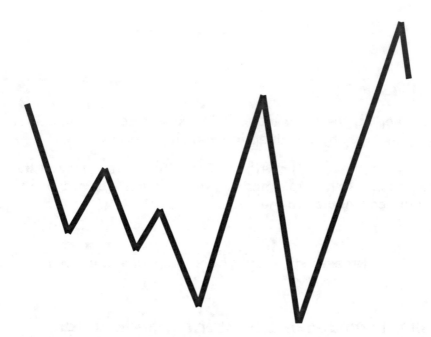

Here's the story arc example we used in the chapter on Writer's Block. The quickening pace is the upbeat; the downbeat is the lessened intensity, the slowing of pace.

Each story has a beginning, middle, and end. I forget who originally said that, but she was right. Pace plays a part throughout the plot, so we can look at each section to see how that works.

I don't like to preach a certain story arc (three-act, five-act, eight-point, and so on) because I find it changes based on the story I'm telling. Secondly, I'm a bit lazy and that seems like a lot to learn. Thirdly, a strict format stifles creativity.

Let's just say that there is a general structure that can and will change based on needs, but the subject of pace holds true no matter how you structure your scenes.

The Beginning (story, chapter, scene)

I like to begin with action. Throw the reader in and get her hooked.

The beginning should put the reader into the plot and allow her to get her bearings then pull her into the middle of the story.

Don't start with a prologue. Yuck. I know some big name authors use prologues, but I'm not a big name author and can't trudge my reader through background I'm too lazy to reveal through snazzy writing. My reader would slam the book closed on me.

Start with action and grab your reader by the eyebrows and don't let go until she is hooked.

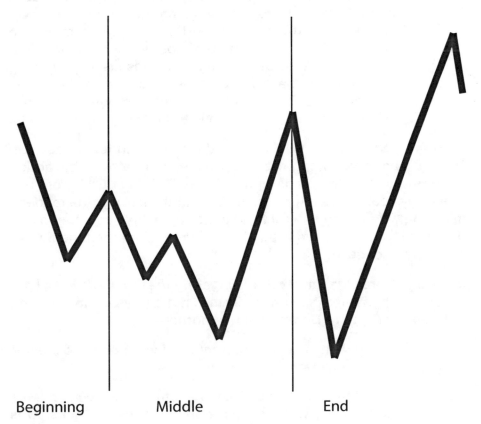

Beginning   Middle   End

The beginning can be either fast and jolting right in the middle of the action or mid-speed with the aftermath of the action. If you go with the aftermath of an action, the reader's mind goes back to fill in the event.

Here's the beginning of my novel *Devil's Bridge*:

> Myra's head ached as she pulled herself up onto the couch. Something warm like melted butter flowed into her right eye, but the stream stung, and her lid fluttered. With a tentative touch, she brushed her eyelid with her hand. Blood covered her fingers. Neither panic nor fear steered Myra's thoughts, only logic: *Damn, I should try to get my contact out.* She held the wall for support and staggered to the bathroom. The harsh, white light from the florescent bulb over the sink made her cringe and brought more pain to the bloody eye. She washed it with water and managed to remove the contact. The bleeding had almost stopped. It was just a slight cut from Gil's Timex. That was his way of being considerate—back-handing her with his left hand. He had never punched her with the full strength of his right arm, just a get-in-line slap with his left.

I didn't need to show Gil's abuse; the reader understands from Myra's actions and thoughts. She's in the aftermath of a big action in her story. I let the reader get to know Myra and Gil before any more physical abuse happens. It stays in the back of the reader's mind, but when they see Gil for the first time, he's apologetic and the man Myra fell in love with. That helps them understand Myra's reluctance to leave.

In my first Derek Mason Mystery *Fingering the Family Jewels*, I put the reader right into the action. This is not a physical movement, but a mental slap to Derek from his mother.

> "Aunt Walt is dead." Mother's voice, strong and steady, struck my ear.
>
> I switched the phone to the other ear. "What? She can't be." Walterene, a cousin of my mother's, was one of the few family members I liked. "I talked to her last week."

"Nonetheless, she died from a sudden stroke."   Her simple statement stung from the lack of emotion, lack of sympathy.

My stomach cramped as if my breath had been knocked out of me by her words. "But..." I struggled to speak. "When?"

"Tuesday night." Mother always was short and direct.

"How's Aunt Ruby?"

"Ruby thought I should call you... Let you know about Walt."

"When is the—"

The phone clicked, followed by silence, then a dial tone. The Bitch had hung up on me. "Damn you." I slammed the phone down.

The pace is quicker in the opening of *Fingering the Family Jewels*. We're in the action with Derek. We hear the conversation. We feel his emotions.

Devil's Bridge opens a little slower, but still showing action. This helps mirror Myra's personality of a thinker and planner.

SUGGESTION: *Open with showing action to start with a quick pace.*

"Showing" quickens the pace; it grabs the reader's attention.

Start "in scene." Show the middle of the action. Do not start with a description: "It was a dark and stormy night." That's telling. The reader can get the description later.

Conflict

Conflict propels the story forward. The characters react to conflict. Each event leads to the next. That's pacing.

Dorothy would never leave Uncle Henry and Aunt Em's farm if there had been no conflict caused by Toto biting Almira Gulch.

How that conflict is paced depends on the type of story you are writing.

Types of stories & pacing

Below are some examples of categories that use distinct pace rates in their genres.

PACING	CATEGORIES OF STORIES
High	Thrillers Mysteries True-Crime
Varied	Romance Westerns Science Fiction Fantasy Historical Biography

	Literary How-To
Low	

High pacing is needed to drive the reader forward in the excitement of the moment. Authors of thrillers and mysteries use a majority of "showing" to quicken the pace. There is some "telling," but the dominate style is showing action, having the reader experience the scenes.

Most genres use a variety of pacing. Description and reflection are important in romances. Certainly science fiction and fantasy stories need time to build and describe the unique worlds in which the stories are set. You have the same need for explaining the yesteryear setting and distinctive culture of historical and western fiction.

Slower paced genres include literary, where the word choice and imagery are paramount more so than the plot, and non-fiction like how-to books, where conveying knowledge is the focus.

Driving Forward

In fiction and some creative non-fiction, authors want the reader to turn the page, to get so involved in the story that chapter breaks are mere speed bumps for bathroom breaks, not stopping points.

SUGGESTION: *Make scenes and chapters end with cliffhangers.*

> Don't give the reader all the information. Leave the reader wanting to go on to learn what happens next.

Not all scenes and chapters can be cliffhangers. You need to let the reader rest at some point, but grab them with your pace and let them ride the roller coaster that is your story arc.

How to do this?

One of the basic ways of showing is to write characters talking and doing things together. Dialog moves the story. The reader is in-the-moment with the characters. She sees the action in her mind as she reads. This creates a movie in the reader's head.

I have to admit that I'm a child of the late 1960s and 1970s. I learned a lot of storytelling techniques from television and movies. My first stories were very third person-outside points of view, a dramatic style like in a stage play or film where little interior dialog is revealed.

When I write, I "see" the action in my head as if I am watching an internal film. I try to capture that on paper. This leads a fast pace and a lot of showing.

My characters don't stop and discuss their feelings very often, but I'm trying to get better at that. I want to be able to use a varied pace to be flexible.

Reflection (telling) slows down the pace and gives the reader a summary that is important to upcoming events. The reader needs this measured, leisurely pace to process all that has happened and to prepare for the drive forward in the plot.

In my novel *Under a Copper Moon*, I made a conscious effort to vary the pace, to bring in a richness to the descriptions and reflection. Here is a beginning scene paragraph from the first chapter with a summary of Inez's predicament:

> Her letters to a cousin in Greenville, an aunt in Charleston, and another cousin in Kershaw didn't receive replies. She considered loading up her trunk of clothes and a few of her mother's books and quilts, packing the wagon, and arriving uninvited on her aunt's doorstep, but the thought of traveling that far, alone, and with an uncertain reception, frightened her more

than staying in the house and surviving on what she could find in the garden. Her few hens had stopped laying eggs on a regular basis; she had fried the rooster, maybe the hens protested that decision. The cow's milk had dried up, and she had exchanged that old cow for the overdue bills at the mercantile. Using her father's rifle, she tracked through the woods and fields searching for rabbits, but once she had one in her sights, she dropped her aim when she saw it had a mate nearby. She couldn't bring herself to widow a rabbit.

(from *Under a Copper Moon* by Greg Lilly)

The scene before this passage was dialog between Inez and a neighbor checking on her well-being. This description of her actual dilemma moves the plot to her next decision, which the reader should be a part of, seeing it play out on the page.

Telling helps transition from one action scene to the next, giving the reader the processing time she needs.

SUGGESTION: *Heartbeat the scenes*

Think of the scenes as one up and one down, like a heartbeat on an electrocardiograph machine. A scene with "showing" goes up in pace and a scene of "telling" brings the pace down.

Two short scenes can give the story a heartbeat: one reflection to one of tension.

Writing – A Visual Art

I think of writing as a visual art. The reader uses his eyes to read the words, sentences, paragraphs, scenes, and chapters. The way those appear on the page subliminally register with a reader.

A page full of thick, dense words is not appealing to a reader. White space — the section of the page without printing — helps the reader organize and process the words he reads.

Consider "show & tell" construction. Showing uses dialog, which looks like this:

> "Why are you always trying to imply something with these paintings?" Maggie Langston stood in Topher's grandmother's kitchen eating cold fried chicken and mashed potatoes over the sink.
>
> Topher watched his mother's face as she surveyed his painting.
>
> "Why don't you paint a picture of your grandmother or a bowl of fruit?"
>
> "You just don't understand. I want to show emotion, hurt, pain—something people can relate to."
>
> His grandmother, who had been sitting at the table smoking a cigarette, offered, "Hell, do like your mama said and paint my picture. I can show you pain. I just think about the time your mama ran off with that good-for-nothing father of yours. He took her to New York, and then runs off with an I-talian gal half his age. Now, that's pain."
>
> "Exactly." Topher moved the painting to face her. "Can't you see that pain in this? I'm trying to convey that same story with these images."
>
> "Christopher," his grandmother shook her head, "try to learn a trade."
>
> (from *Devil's Bridge* by Greg Lilly)

With description or exposition, you are telling and it tends to be longer paragraphs and looks like this:

> Inside the house, Ruby was napping, so I stood on the deck and watched the Gambel's Quail scurry through the brush with their fuzzy, walnut-sized babies following. The birds seemed to have a better family structure than most humans. An adult quail would navigate the way with the offspring lined up behind them while, another adult rallied the end of the train, keeping stragglers on course. I had seen them hurry across the road in front of my car before, one male stopping in the middle of the pavement to glare at me until all the birds made it across safely, before darting off the road like a hyper crossing guard. With Ruby alone and moving two thousand miles from North Carolina, I felt like it was my turn to guide her after all the years she had taken care of me. Maybe this newly emerging sense of responsibility was amplified by the confusion about my relationship with Daniel, or the tension I still felt with Mark, or the hurt that lingered with my mother and the rest of the family. We were no quails. Our family was emotionally scattered in all directions, with no one trying to keep us together.
>
> (from *Scalping the Red Rocks — a Derek Mason Mystery* by Greg Lilly)

Just by glancing at the two samples, you tend to start reading the shorter sentences and paragraphs. A block of text seems imposing.

How a
page of
"**showing**"
text might
look to a
reader.

How a page of **"telling"** text tends to run together for a reader.

SUGGESTION: *Visual inspection*

Step back from the page and conduct a visual inspection.

Does the page look inviting to the eye?

Is there more text or white space?

Does the manuscript consistently show thick paragraphs, short sentences, short or long scenes, or choppy chapters?

This is a good way to make sure you vary the structure of your words, sentences, paragraphs, scenes, and chapters.

Rhythm

The visual inspection illustrates the visual *rhythm* to the page. Too many short sentences and paragraphs look choppy. Too many long sentences and paragraphs look inflated or bulky.

Not only is there a visual rhythm, there is an audio rhythm, whether read aloud or in your head.

SUGGESTION: *Read your manuscript out loud.*

Listen to the rhythm of the words and sentences. Are you using a lot of short words in short sentences? Does it sound like you are bumping over train tracks as you read? Vary the sentence structure and think like a poet with your word choice.

The rhythm extends to the scenes and chapters as well. Short scenes and chapters keep the reader moving forward. A well-known thriller writer explained how he likes to write short scenes and chapters. How often, he asked, do you flip ahead to see how many pages are left before a break. If it is too many, you stop there. If it is just one more page, you keep reading. That is his trick to keep the reader involved: frequent breaks for the reader, but each scene or chapter change also creates a "turn."

Turns

A "turn" in the story is a conflict that pushes the characters forward. Let's look to our Bubble Graph from the chapter on Writer's Block.

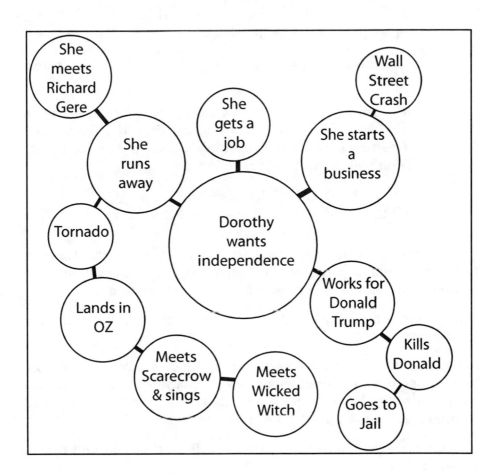

Each bubble is a turn in the story; it's a new conflict that propels Dorothy forward.

Rhythm & Pace

To increase the pace of an intense action scene, use short sentences with active verbs. This creates a quick, breath-taking pace. Here is a sample:

> She glanced at her watch. Only ten minutes. It seemed like an hour. A Jeep Cherokee pulled into the lot and parked at the corner of the building, obstructing her view.

"Damn it. I'm going in."

She crept to the Cherokee and peeked at Gil's truck. Empty.

He was still inside the pawn shop. *What if this sets him off? He might think I'm spying on him... Well, I am. He's been so sweet and kind lately, I should just go. Damn, Tina's in there. Come on, Tina. Let's go.*

(from *Devil's Bridge* by Greg Lilly)

Pace parallels what is at stake for the characters, the tension. The more tension you have, the more you will naturally shorten your sentences, using shorter words and action verbs.

Trust your storytelling abilities. The pace will build as the excitement builds.

Pace needs to be balanced: action and recovery/reflection. Remember the heartbeat of pace. A chapter is like running a race; a novel is like running a marathon. You can't go full-speed all the time. We all need a bit of recovery time.

But, we have to keep moving forward. (I tend to like fast paced writing.)

TIPS:

- Start the chapter "In Scene" not with description
- Active verbs, not passive
- Keep the conflicts coming
- Short sentences, scenes, chapters

Books I like on pace:

- *Show, Don't Tell* by William Noble

- *Word Painting* by Rebecca McClanahan

Snagging a Publisher

Whether targeting a publisher or a literary agent with your manuscript, you will need a kit of sales documents called the Query Packet ready to submit.

Reminder

The process:

1. Write your book (only non-fiction allows you to query with an outline and a sample of an unfinished manuscript)

2. Revise & edit your book

3. Have another person read it (first readers)

4. Polish until you think it is perfect

5. Craft the query packet (as important as the manuscript)

    • This is your "sales packet"

    • This can be as hard as writing the novel

        ° Examine what you've written

        ° Dissect it

        ° Get to its core

        ° Summarize hundreds of pages into one compelling paragraph

        ° And do it well enough that it stands out among the hundreds of others that agents and editors receive

The Query Packet

QUERY? WHAT'S A QUERY?

You're asking an agent to represent your work to a publisher (or if you are querying a publisher directly, you're asking them to publish your work).

WHAT MAKES UP A QUERY PACKET?

Check with the publisher or agent's website to see what they want a writer to send them to evaluate your query. Most use all or a subset of these.

- **Elevator Pitch** – one to three sentences that excite your audience (used in your Query letter)

- **Synopsis** – a concise, but entertaining summary of your manuscript

- **Query Letter** – the introduction letter, the first contact you have with agent or editor to sell your manuscript and yourself as a writer

WHO TO QUERY? PUBLISHER OR AGENT?

- Some larger publishers only accept queries from agents
- Agents act as a filter for large publishers
- Agents get 10 to 20% of what you earn
- **WARNING:** some "agents" charge reading fees or other fees
  - An agent makes money from selling manuscripts, not reading, not editing, not referring you to their in-house editing service
  - **NEVER** pay an agent

- Small publishing houses usually allow writers to query them directly
- Check their website for Submission Guidelines (and follow them)

TERMINOLOGY:

- **eQueries** — queries sent via e-mail. These involve all the same elements as you use in a Query packet, just send them with e-mail. This is becoming very popular. Some agencies and publishers do not accept U.S. mail queries, only eQueries.

- **Simultaneous Queries?** – Depends on their response times. I suggest sending simultaneous queries, but if you get a request for the full manuscript, give exclusivity for reading the manuscript to that agent. But, make sure there is a time limit — like three weeks. If they don't respond within three weeks, you can send the manuscript to someone else.

- **SASE** stands for Self-Addressed Stamped Envelope. Make sure the envelope is large enough to return your materials and has the correct postage. You must use stamps. A metered label is only good for the day it is printed — do not use one.

OTHER TIPS:

- Read or investigate the books they publish — the number one rejection reason is that the manuscript doesn't fit the list. *This wastes everyone's time and is a sure sign of an amateur.*

- Writing is both craft and art. Know the mechanics of punctuation, grammar, and self-editing.

Step 1 — Finish Your Fiction Manuscript

Before querying an agent or publisher, your fiction manuscript must be complete.

"Complete" means draft, revise, polish, work with a critique group and first readers, revise, reread, revise, ask more people to read it, revise...repeat until you are sick of the manuscript.

Take critiques with grace. Determine what advice to use and what to let go. Learn self-editing.

SUGGESTION:

> Read *Self-Editing for Fiction Writers — How to Edit Yourself into Print*
>
> by Renni Browne & Dave King

Step 2 — Create Your Pitch

What's your novel about? If you had 20 seconds, could you explain the heart of the story and grab someone's interest?

This is important, because you need to be able to explain the story in its simplest form, in one powerful sentence.

The simplest form to do this is:

(***Character***) wants (***goal***) because (***motivation***), but faces (***conflict***).

EXAMPLE:

George, a young squirrel, wants to raid the bird feeder to impress his girlfriend, but a greased pole blocks his path.

Pitch Worksheet

1	The title of your novel:
2	Your main character's name:
3	A few words that describe your character:
4	What does your character want to accomplish? (goal)

5	Why does the character want to accomplish this goal? (motivation)
6	What stands in the way of the character achieving this goal? (conflict)
7	Using these answers, write a one to three sentence description of what the novel is about. This is your pitch.

EXAMPLES:

Love on the Big Screen by William J. Torgerson

> In the novel *Love on the Big Screen*, Zuke, a college freshman whose understanding of love has been shaped by late-eighties romantic comedies, chases romance, only to discover real love is not a John Hughes movie.

Devil's Bridge by Greg Lilly

> In *Devil's Bridge*, two friends, Topher and Myra, find strength in each other to leave their old lives for a new beginning — if her husband doesn't track them down first.

Jaws by Peter Benchley

> *Jaws* is a story about New England sheriff who is afraid of the ocean. When a great white shark terrorizes and kills tourists swimming at his beach, he has to face his greatest fear and go out to sea to catch and kill the shark. Eventually the boat is sunk, the crew lost and the sheriff and the shark have a final and fatal showdown in the water.

There are variations using some or all the same elements of Character — Goal — Motivation — Conflict.

What if...

Start with "What if" then add the premise of the book, the kernel that caught your imagination.

> What if the Wicked Witch of the West had a history with Glenda, the Good Witch of the North? (*Wicked*)

The Hollywood Pitch

This is sometimes called the series of threes with a surprise at the end:

A story about the first man, the first woman, and the sneaky snake that tore them apart. (Genesis, *The Bible*)

A story about a hidden lynching, a secret love, an unholy union, and the misfit son who might expose them all. (*Fingering the Family Jewels*)

EXERCISE:

Create the Pitch for your novel using the *Pitch Worksheet* on page 59.

Keep it handy because we'll use it again.

Step 3 — Write the Synopsis

The Synopsis is a concise selling tool for your novel, a summary meant to make an editor want to read your manuscript.

A synopsis should:

- be written in present tense

- contain your opening Pitch

- include quick sketches of the main characters (woven into your narrative)

- highlight the core conflict

- illustrate plot high points

- include the conclusion

A synopsis lays out the plot of your novel for the editor so she can see your storytelling structure. It's not meant to be an example of your writing.

Open with your Pitch. This should draw in the editor to want to read the synopsis.

Detail the beginning and ending with one or two middle scenes that give an idea of kind of emotional intensity or the type of action to be expected.

If your story contains graphic sex or violence, it should be obvious from the synopsis.

Summarize the rest in short, tight paragraphs with strong action verbs and few descriptive adjectives and adverbs.

The character's physical descriptions are not vital, but their motivations are.

Use dialogue only for occasional emphasis.

Make sure every loose end is tied up — never leave an editor guessing about anything.

TIPS:
- Use the same writing style and tone that you use in your novel: chatty & upbeat, dark & brooding, etc. A flat synopsis

reflects a flat novel.

- Try to keep it to one page, or two at the most.

- Don't end with a cliffhanger. A synopsis must include the novel's ending.

- Write tight: limit adjectives and adverbs; avoid the temptation to include every scene and background detail.

Synopsis Worksheet

1	The title of your novel:
2	Write the PITCH for your book (from the previous worksheet):
3	Write character sketches for each major characters. Focus on the characters' motivations, especially what brings them into conflict with each other.

4	List the plot highlights. Begin by detailing the beginning and ending scenes and one or two from the middle.
	These plot points are the necessary ones to illustrate the structure of the primary plot. Include the ending to show how the plot's conflict is wrapped up.

5	Using the above information, outline your novel synopsis, paragraph by paragraph.
	You may use your own structure, but make sure all the elements of the synopsis are addressed:
	• an opening Pitch
	• quick sketches of the main characters
	• plot high points
	• the core conflict
	• the conclusion

Step 4 — Compose the Query Letter

WHAT IS A QUERY LETTER?

- It's the carrot dangled in front of an agent or publisher to get them to move.

- It's the "profile" of your lonely manuscript in the publisher-dating world.

- A query letter must "Sell" your idea of your novel or book idea to an editor or agent so that person will give you permission to submit your manuscript, or at least a few chapters for further consideration.

- A query letter represents your novel and you by listing what your novel is about, who you are, the length of the manuscript, and why you chose to submit to this person.

WHAT A QUERY LETTER *CAN* DO:

- Help your work rise above the slush pile

WHAT A QUERY LETTER *CAN'T* DO:

- Sell a poor manuscript

WHAT A QUERY LETTER *SHOULD* DO:

- Pitch your work to an editor
- Entice the editor to want to see your work
- Sell your idea

THE ELEMENTS OF A QUERY LETTER

- The pitch
- The handle
- A mini-synopsis
- Your credentials
- Your credits
- What you're offering
- The closing

The query letter is the first thing an agent or publisher will see when she/he opens the Query Packet.

It must make the person want to keep reading to move on to the synopsis, and then to read your sample pages...And then to ask to see the full manuscript! That's your goal.

Let's take a look at each element that makes up this first selling tool: The query letter.

The *Pitch:*

- Created in Step 2's worksheet on page 59.

The *Handle*:

- Gives the reader something to hold onto

- Something to help the reader determine if they can sell your book

- Identifies your novel's theme (e.g. unrequited love)

- Compares your novel to other novels – what it's like; what's already out there and selling

- Any information to support that your novel has a niche and will sell

EXAMPLE:

  While *Revenge for Old Times' Sake* is a fast-paced, madcap mystery, with rich characterizations, it also aims a powerful skewer at the arena of tabloid TV.

A *Mini-Synopsis*:

- Presents an overview of the plot

- Introduces your main characters and their core conflict

- Include a few high points

- Make the setting and time period

Create the Mini-Synopsis by boiling down your Synopsis written in Step 3's worksheet on page 65.

Your *Credentials*:

- Who are you? (Give a little information about yourself.)

- How did you come to write this novel? (Convey knowledge of your subject matter.)

Your *Credits*:

- Shows you have a track record; others have found your work acceptable; you are a professional who has experience working with editors

- If you are not published, don't bring attention to it in a negative way

- List fiction credits and nonfiction credits

What You're Offering:

- List: title, word count, genre

- Know what kind of book you have written

- If you don't know the category, you may leave it out – comparing to another book can help the editor/agent decide what category it might fall in

The *Closing*:

- You may make a brief reference to the publisher's guidelines

- "I noticed in your writer's guidelines that you prefer to see a one-page synopsis and the first three chapters rather than the full manuscript. May I send you a synopsis and my first three chapters?"

- If the guidelines don't specify what to send, offer to send your COMPLETE manuscript:

  - "May I send my complete manuscript?"

  - "May I send you my completed 90,000-word mainstream novel [title]?"

- Thank the editors/agents for their time/consideration

Query Letter Worksheet

1	The title of your novel:
2	How many words is your novel? (word count)

3	What is your novel's genre?
4	To what other novel(s) is your novel similar?
5	What is your novel's theme?
6	Where is the story set?
7	In what time period is your novel set and what is duration of time?

8	State the PITCH of your novel (from your Pitch Worksheet, page 59).
9	Why did you write this novel? (Special knowledge of the subject matter, special setting, or knowledge of a profession)
10	List any fiction credits you have. (If you have no fiction credits, but have substantial non-fiction credits, you might mention those, especially if they have relevance to the world you've created in your novel.)

11	Beginning with your main character, list your primary characters and their core conflicts in the novel (especially your main character's). Include a brief description of each, but most importantly, identify their roles in the novel's plot.

12	What are the "high points" (plot points) of your novel?
	(These are only the points that must be included to tell your story. If one point is excluded, the story would not be the same. Start with three points and only add those that are absolutely necessary, trying to have no more than six.)

MORE QUERY LETTER TIPS

- Keep it brief. One interesting, intriguing, informative page should do it.

- The style of your query should reflect the style of your novel.

- Include word count.

- Don't say you write like a particular best-selling author. Rather say you write in the same genre as that author or in a similar style.

- Don't mention how many people "have read and loved my novel."

- Exclude self-glorifying adjectives (dazzling, dramatic, exciting, fast-paced, etc.).

- Don't predict your book's climb up the best-seller lists.

- Propose only one project per query. You may mention, however, if you plan a series.

- Don't put yourself down.

- Don't tell the editor or agent his/her business.

- Be polite. Don't discuss an advance, rights, or make demands.

- Don't show desperation.

Query Letter Checklist

Before mailing out a query letter, check over it for the following elements that can lead to rejection:

- ☐ Weak opening sentence

- ☐ Wordiness

- ☐ Awkward phrasing

- ☐ Lack of clarity

- ☐ Illogical paragraph organization

- ☐ Repetitiveness

- ☐ Weak verbs

- ☐ Clichés

- ☐ Lack of rhythm

- ☐ Overusing adjectives and adverbs

- ☐ No transitions, or weak transitions, between paragraphs

- ☐ Weak plotting, as related in the query

- ☐ Incorrect punctuation, grammar, and spelling

- ☐ Include your name, address, phone number, e-mail and a list of publishing credits (if you have any)

- ☐ For U.S. Mail, include a SASE (Self-Addressed Stamped Envelope)

Query Letter Examples

Dear XXXX,

In 1903, the New York Post branded Jerome, Arizona the "Wickedest Town in America." What would a young girl encounter in that mining town during the decade leading up to this notorious label? From mine explosions, rowdy men, and enterprising prostitutes to Chinese slavery, opium dens, and a lonely sheriff, Inez fights her way to independence and respect.

Pitch

In my novel, *INEZ—Portrait of a Mail-Order Bride*, a young woman finds herself alone and hopeless when her mother dies, then she discovers adventure in a newspaper ad. After a long train ride across the country, Inez meets her future husband who paid for her trip to Jerome in the Arizona Territory. Their plans are destroyed when a mining accident kills her husband-to-be. Again, Inez finds herself on her own and her prospects bleak until she encounters the ladies of Onalee's parlor house.

Mini-synopsis

INEZ is story of grit, daring, perseverance and a splash of Lady Marmalade in the late Victorian era when men were strong and women were supposed to be coy and quiet... But no one could convince Inez of that.

Handle /
Hollywood
Pitch

I am the author of *FINGERING THE FAMILY JEWELS* and *DEVIL'S BRIDGE* (to be published in May 2007). Also, my short fiction is included in the anthology *WOMEN BEHAVING BADLY.*

Credits

This historical fiction manuscript is outside the list of my current publisher, so I am seeking representation to find a suitable publishing house. May I send you a copy of the 68,000 word manuscript?

What I'm offering and a call to action

Thank you for your time and consideration. I look forward to hearing from you.

Closing

Sincerely,

Greg Lilly

Full Contact Information

450 Last Wagon Drive
Sedona, AZ 86336

928-204-1641

Greg@GregLilly.com
www.GregLilly.com

Listing your website and a "professional e-mail" are a slick way to show you know how to market yourself and your books.

Note on e-mail addresses:

> Create a professional writer's e-mail to use for your query. Best case, secure your own website and set

the e-mail up through it. Otherwise, create a simple gmail or yahoo or other free account that says you are a professional. *yourname*@gmail.com

Personal e-mails like SkylarsMom@aol.com, SexyFifi@yahoo.com, and GunsNGuts@gmail.com send the wrong message to prospective agents and publishers.

Good & Not-So-Good Examples

With query letters, as in life, it is sometimes useful to see examples of what **not** to do.

Let's take a look at some really misguided attempts to grab attention. These did grab attention, but not in the way the writer wanted.

Disclaimer:

> The following examples are real query letters we received at Cherokee McGhee Publishing. Names and details have been changed to protect identities, but the intent and tone remain.

QUERY LETTER EXAMPLE — REJECTED

575 B Street
Sudbury, CA 94586

Dear Sir or Madam:

My name is John Smith, I am a new and as yet
unpublished writer but everyone started out this
way, including J. K. Rowlings, Dan Brown and
Stephen King. It is my goal to become a mem-
ber of this illustrious group.

> He's compar-
> ing himself
> to bestselling
> authors.
>
> A bit arrogant.
>
> Let me decide
> how good you
> are.

My only qualifications at the present time are
that I have been an avid reader since I was six,
mentally devouring nearly every piece of writing
I could get my hands on and that I seem to have
the ability to tell interesting and exciting stories.
Last but by no means least, rejection does not
phase me, it only makes me more determined to
succeed.

> Good. It's
> nice to know
> that he
> understands
> the business.

I know that for a first novel to be successful, it
needs to be more than an interesting, well written story. Marketing and promotion are no doubt
the most important things. While my marketing
knowledge is limited, I do have a few ideas that
could possibly help in this department.

> He seems
> set on an
> expensive
> cover and
> could be
> difficult to work
> with.

When it comes to the presentation aspect, I
have the concept for a book cover that will blow
the competition out of the water. Not only will it
attract immediate attention but I believe it will
make my young adult novel *Maid of the Word*,
(167,555 words) an instant collector's item.

> 167,000 words
> is 100,000 too
> many.

Maid of the Word is more than an exciting adventure; it is also the story about the growth and maturity of two self centered teens, Jack and Megan. Jack becomes a master archer and Megan a fierce warrior. Their friendship and loyalty are tested to the breaking point and beyond.
A test they both pass with flying colors. By the time they reach the end of their perilous journey they are willing to give up their lives for each other and for their friends.

Because I believe that my novel is a perfect fit for your publishing house, with your permission I would like to submit it for you to evaluate.

Sincerely
John Smith
Email: JS@yahoo.com

Phone: 705-555-0786

PS: At the present time there is a reader vacuum created by the ending of the Harry Potter series of books, I firmly believe that my book can and will fill this void. I know that if we work together on this project with the intention of making this book a success it will be a huge one, making us both a great deal of money. I am willing to do my part, are you?

Nice mini-synopsis.

What? Why is it a "perfect fit"?

Good. I need the name and contact information.

Oh, no... Forget the P.S.

This tone is "trouble" even if the partials were awesome, I would hesitate working with him.

Query Letter Example — REJECTED

August 8, 2012

From: Mary Jones. Address 12345 Strauss Avenue Selden, NY 11784: Telephone Number/Fax: 301-555-6497. E-mail: MaryJones@gmail.com

To: The Editors Cherokee McGhee L.L.C.:

Thanks for taking the time to review my work. I'm a published author with several books on the market and a few more due for release next year. Writing has always been a part of my life, but for the past seven years, I've worked, extensively, on cultivating this craft. My novel, *Broken Dishes*, collection of poetry, *Words on Fire vol 1*, are currently available through major bookstores. Two novels are due for release next year, *A Path Through the Cellar* and *A Distant View*. I am submitting my novel, *Light Piercing Through Shadows* for your review. This novel is about 136,000 words in length and can be categorized as Inspirational Romance.

Since my teenage years, I've been an avid reader of romance novels. In fact, the influence of these books, have given me a sense for this style of writing. Because of my faith, I'm able to communicate the romance genre, from a Christian perspective. Seven years ago, I left my position as an Elementary School Teacher and started writing on a full-time basis.

So, more than any experience I may have had, I know it's my calling and destiny to be a writer. In my youth, I worked with community magazines,

Good, put that you are published at the beginning. Helps you stand out.

It would help to know who the publishers are and why they don't want this new book.

A 136,000 word novel shows a lack of self-editing.

This doesn't tell me anything I need to know about the submission.

Youth Mix-Up, Maranatha Zeel Magazine, and *Point of View Magazine*. I was both author and editor to these blossoming journals, and they served as stepping stones to my fulfilling my potential.

"Light Piercing Through Shadows," concerns the life of a Steve Landers, a Pastor who loses his wife to cancer and left to raise three small children on his own. The deep and lasting wound of the loss, causes him to make a vow to never open up his heart to love again. But, months later, when he and his children vacation at a Summer house in Florida, he meets a wonderful and special woman, Sandy Lee, who makes him feel alive again. This woman loves him, but even if he develops feelings for her. because of unresolved guilt, associated with his wife's death, he puts up a defensive wall, which subsequently drives her away.

Eventually, they find their way back to each other, but their love is acutely challenged, when critical members from Steve's church, disapproves of his relationship with Sandy and endeavors to destroy his reputation in the community, as a Pastor. They go to great lengths, in order to have Steve expelled from the church, he's founded. Steve is left to make a pivotal choice between remaining true to his church, or remaining true to the woman he loves. This account deals with the trials both the hero and heroine encounter in their lives, on the rocky road, leading to their ride off into the sunset...

Nice mini-synopsis, but a few punctuation & editing problems. Makes me wonder what editing issues are in the 136,000 word manuscript.

Overall, not bad. The partial was well-written, but the subject matter (Christian Romance) does not fit my list.

Now, on to some queries that were done well.

Following are examples of what you should do with a query letter...

Query Letter Example — Accepted

Dear Greg:

REVENGE FOR OLD TIMES' SAKE is the third adventure in the multi-award-winning and nominated Tracy Eaton mystery series.

Free-spirited Tracy cheers when her stuffy husband, Drew, loosens up enough to rearrange the nose of his secretive boss, Ian Dragger. But Drew's timing couldn't be worse. When Ian is found floating face down in the Eatons' pool, Drew is the one that wily Detective Fay Cardinale zeroes in on as her prime suspect. Yet Ian made enemies like the mint makes money, and other suspects abound, starting with Ian's wife, progressive Kathy Right, who was nearly as at odds with her husband's affluent lifestyle as she was the affair he might have been having at the time of his death. And sleazy journalist Nick Wickerson, of "Nick Wick's Sin City" TV fame, whom Ian humiliated in court.

Still, Tracy expects to clear Drew in short order. But that's before help arrives — in the form of her own mother, over-the-top movie actress Martha Collins, and her rigid-with-dignity mother-in-law, Charlotte Eaton. And when the mothers get together, the fireworks go off. Obstacles mount higher still when Drew's ex-flame, attorney CeeCee Payne, deals herself into the game. But CeeCee's peculiar behavior raises too many questions. Does she want Drew back? Or is CeeCee's after revenge, since her actions threaten to condemn him to a life behind bars.

When the bodies in the Eaton pool start stacking up like timber in a logging camp, Tracy knows that nothing less than her wildest antics will do. But as the blows keep coming Drew's way, she

Nice to know it is a series and this is # 3.

She's experienced.

She's won awards.

Nice entertaining synopsis.

Mimics the tone of the manuscript.

Think of this as your book cover summary. It serves the same purpose and a version of it usually ends up being used for that.

fears that even her craziness won't be enough to save him.

While REVENGE FOR OLD TIMES' SAKE is a fast-paced, madcap mystery, with rich characterizations, it also aims a powerful skewer at the arena of tabloid TV.

The series includes REVENGE OF THE GYPSY QUEEN, an Agatha, Anthony and Macavity Award-nominee (the first and only small press book to have ever garnered the triple crown of mystery fiction award nominations), DEM BONES' REVENGE, a Samantha Award winner, and the short stories, "L.A. Justice," a Derringer Award winner, "Murder, 90201," "Malibu Dreamin'."

Mystery News has written: "Kris Neri and Tracy Eaton will be favorites in the mystery field for quite a long time." For other reviews, see: http://www.krisneri.com/gq-reviews.html and http://www.krisneri.com/dbr-reviews.html.

This series enjoys a wide readership — all of the award nominations garnered by REVENGE OF THE GYPSY QUEEN are reader awards. Fans keep emailing to ask for more adventures featuring Tracy and the gang. I'm prepared to build on this sizeable base in marketing this book.

I am also the author of the standalone thriller, NEVER SAY DIE and THE ROSE IN THE SNOW, a short story collection, as well as sixty short stories.

For my full bio, see my website.

Following my signature are a short synopsis and a 50-page partial.

Cordially,
Kris

Awards & other books in the series.

blurbs

A following and a built-in audience.

Also shows she can market her books.

Her 50-page sample kept me turning the pages and laughing out loud (in a good way). That sold it.

--
Kris Neri
http://www.krisneri.com

REVENGE FOR OLD TIMES' SAKE SYNOPSIS:

Even stodgy, blueblood lawyers, like Tracy's husband, Drew, have their limits. Drew's boss, trial lawyer Ian Dragger, had been riding Drew throughout the trial to free ribald comic-turned-secular televangelist, Skippy Sullivan. Skippy, an old nemesis of Tracy's movie star mother, and the organization he'd formed, DOLT, Decency and Order in Life and on TV, had been charged with raiding the set of Scarlet Stories, a tabloid TV show. Drew celebrates Skippy's unexpected acquittal by popping Ian in the nose. Too bad the next time anyone saw Ian, he was floating in the Eaton swimming pool, deader than disco.

Wiley detective Fay Cardinale is nobody's fool, but Drew makes too good a suspect for her to look any farther. Even though Ian made enemies like the mint makes money, and other suspects abound. Starting with Ian's wife, progressive Kathy Right, who was nearly as at odds with her husband's affluent lifestyle as she was the affair he might have been having. And smarmy journalist Nick Wickerson, of Nick Wick's Sin City TV fame.

Others raise questions, too. Such as Vanessa Eccerly, a gawky, pink-haired publicist to Tracy's mother, Martha Collins, who doesn't have any obvious ability for PR, but who seems awfully noisy about the Eaton household. And Riley Jacks, the juror credited with freeing Skippy Sullivan.

Tracy's convinced the only one without a motive to kill Ian is Skippy Sullivan, since Skippy must have been thrilled with an acquittal no one expected Ian to win.

Drew is jailed for Ian's murder. Still, Tracy expects to clear him in short order. But that's before help arrives — in form of her own mother and her rigid-with-dignity mother-in-law, Charlotte Eaton. And when the mothers get together, the fireworks go off. Even worse, Drew's old flame, attorney CeeCee Payne, the prosecutor on the Sullivan case, comes to his rescue, threatening to break up Tracy's happy home in the process of clearing Drew. Does CeeCee have romance on her mind, or revenge, for Drew's having dropped her years before to marry Tracy?

Attacks against Drew in prison cause Tracy and the family to break him out of custody, disguising him and hiding him in the old money Norman Club, the last place the police would think to look. Yet Tracy remains no closer to solving the crime.

Then Riley Jacks is found dead floating in the Eaton pool. Tracy and Martha stash Riley's body in, first a freezer, and then an unused radio studio, hiding his murder from the police Unfortunately, Vanessa and Charlotte learn what Tracy and Martha did.

The truth about Vanessa comes out. She's not a publicist, but a reporter wannabe, trying to dig up enough dirt about Martha to win a job on Scarlet Stories. Vanessa agrees to sit on Drew's jailbreak and Riley's murder, if Tracy will provide her with a better story later. When Tracy discovers Vanessa had been using a secret spy camera to capture shots around the house, she remembers that it's exactly like one Riley Jacks had worn.

Photos from Riley's mini camera show that Ian paid CeeCee to throw the Sullivan trial, and paid Riley to influence the other members of the jury.

Once Tracy realizes Riley must have told Skippy precisely how his acquittal was engineered, she understands how enraged Skippy would have been with Ian, who made a mockery of his grand gesture. Skippy killed Ian, and later Riley, and dumped them in her pool to get back at Martha. But Tracy can't prove it.

They set up a sting to trap Skippy. But Skippy has an advantage that Tracy knows nothing about. His young wife, Bambi, works at the Norman Club and was on duty when Drew was hidden there. Skippy abducts Drew and blackmails Tracy into meeting him and Bambi at the empty radio studio where they deposited Riley's body.

When Tracy meets Skippy and Bambi at the studio, Riley's body is still propped up before the engineering board, precisely where they left him. When she's forced to enter the room where Skippy is holding Drew, Tracy stumbles into Riley's arm.

Then Bambi tricks Skippy, trapping him in that studio with Tracy, Drew and the departed Riley, just as an extermination crew tents the building to begin termite extermination. As the exterminator prepares to pump poison into the old building, believing it to be empty, Tracy encourages Skippy to talk. When she hit Riley's arm, she engaged the board, so everything said in that studio goes out over the airwaves. That broadcast not only informs Tracy's family of her whereabouts, but also the police, who hear Skippy's confession. The police and Tracy's cohorts arrive at the studio in time to stop the extermination, and to arrest Skippy and Bambi.

Both Drew and his stodgy mother have learned that loosening up is a good thing, even if they can't handle freedom quite as well as Tracy and Martha.

This synopsis example by mystery writer Kris Neri shows that a synopsis should mimic the manuscript's tone and, even in a mystery, the plot ending must be revealed.

This makes me want to read the samples.

QUERY LETTER EXAMPLE — ACCEPTED

Dear Editor:

Enclosed is a synopsis and an excerpt from Fortune Island, my recently completed novel set primarily on the Outer Banks of North Carolina. Jessie Judas, the main character, grows up poor, uneducated, and neglected on the Outer Banks shortly after WWII. With great odds against her, including a dark criminal stain, she becomes a renowned marine biologist. Two levels of story—one moving across the last year of her life and the other moving forward from her birth to catch up to this last year—reveal the dark and dangerous underpinnings of her unhappy inner life and how they coexist with her illustrious public career.

My first novel, *Paradise Square,* was awarded the **Grand Prize for Fiction** from the *International eBook Award Foundation* at the Frankfurt Book Fair in 2000. *Scenario for Scorsese* followed and both are published by Denlinger's Publishers, Ltd. in paperback.   Prior to the novels, poetry had been my chief work and it has appeared in many literary quarterlies here and abroad: everything from The American Scholar to The Yale Review. My prize-winning collection, *Murderer's Day*, was published by Purdue University Press.

Good mini-synopsis and hook. I want to read more.

Impressive awards and publication history.

I hope you'll find this sample intriguing and want to read the whole story.

Sincerely,
E.M. Schorb

http://www.emschorb.com

This is a short letter, but his opening and his experience got me to read his synopsis and partial.

His 50-page writing sample sealed the deal.

The Standard Submission Process at an Agency or Publisher

The literary agent or the publishing house acquisitions editor will list the procedures to submit a manuscript for consideration on the agency/publisher website.

Read and follow these procedures.

Really.

If a prospective author cannot read and follow directions, then that sets the tone for what she/he will be like to work with.

Publishing is a business. Writing is an art & craft. But, publishing is a business.

Many agents and publishing houses will automatically reject any query packet that does not follow the guidelines.

Yes, I know that's not nice, and they should be more *creative*.

But, publishing is a business.

What is publishing?

That's right. It is a business.

Each literary agency or publishing house will have their own procedure, but in general, the chart on the next page shows the flow of the decision making process.

You want to make it through each step.

The Process

(GIVE OR TAKE A LITTLE...HERE OR THERE)

FOLLOW THE PARTICULAR GUIDELINES POSTED BY THE AGENT OR PUBLISHER

Each piece of the query packet gives more detailed information on the manuscript, but it also is a step where the manuscript can be rejected. Make each step riveting and it leaves them asking for more.

Query Letter
 	
Pitch
 	
Mini-Synopsis
	Is the Pitch intriguing?
	
	  YES, I'll keep reading...
	
	  NO -- REJECT the Query.
	
	Is the Mini-Synopsis interesting and original?
	
	  YES, I'll keep reading...
	
	  NO -- REJECT the Query.

Synopsis	Let's see how this writer develops the plot.
	
	  CLEVER? I'll keep reading...
	
	  CONFUSING? -- REJECT the Query.

Sample Pages	Great pitch. Original concept. Well-crafted plot... Can this writer write?
	
	  YES, send me the entire manuscript.
	
	  NO -- REJECT the Query.

Stepping Out — Publication

There are a lot of tasks that come once your manuscript is accepted by a publisher for publication.

Technology changes these on a monthly, if not weekly, basis. So, I will not try to give specifics, but some universal recommendations where you, as an author, should have some control.

The Publishing Contract

Read the contract before you sign it. If you know a lawyer or paralegal, you may want that person to take a look. Most contracts should be understandable by a lay person.

Rights

The right to publish your manuscript is what the contract is about. Other "rights" are usually listed as well.

With Cherokee McGhee, I believe the company should contract for any rights that use the work we've completed on a manuscript: mainly editing and design or the physical result of our labor. So, we ask for print rights in paper and electronic.

Other media such as audio, merchandising, and film, may use the final product that our editors helped shape, but there will be a lot more work involved to prepare the story for a screenplay. We have no hand in that, so I wouldn't ask for the rights to it.

Any rights not directly related to the product of the physical book should be left to the author. That's my view.

SUGGESTION: *Don't sign away "all rights"*

> Check the contract to ensure that you are granting the rights for the book, not for other forms of the story the publisher doesn't intend to use like film, audio, or merchandising.
>
> Any rights not addressed in the contract should be retained by the author. Check for a statement such as:
>
> > *All rights not specifically granted to Publisher in this contract should be deemed reserved by the Author.*

Right of First Refusal

Usually the publisher will want to review any sequel to the book before the author queries other publishers. The publisher has spent a lot of time and money shaping your book, and sequels should be offered to that publisher first.

They may not sign the next book, especially if the characters go in a different direction in tone or actions than the original book, but it's standard to let them have first crack at the new manuscript.

This is for any sequel, not for *any book* you may write afterwards. The contract is for the book, not for you.

Negotiate out any clause that the publisher gets first right of refusal on your next book that is not related to this one.

Author Discount

The contract should list how much of a discount the author receives on books she purchases for her own use, maybe for publicity or to sell at book signing events.

SUGGESTION: *40-50% off the cover price for author purchases*

Royalty

Negotiate any mention of "net proceeds" royalties. This mean that your royalty will change based on how much the book sells for.

The easiest way for a publisher and for an author to calculate royalties is based on cover (or retail) price. That's the cost on the back of the book. It doesn't matter that Amazon might discount the book, that discount will not affect your royalty.

SUGGESTION: *Ask for royalty based on retail price.*

> A standard royalty rate is 10% of retail price, higher if the book sells more than a certain number of copies.

Date of Publication

I have heard horror stories from authors who have signed a publishing contract without a "Publication Date" clause. The book is delayed from publication for one reason or another for years.

This clause ensure that a contractual agreement is set that your manuscript becomes a book by a certain date. Otherwise, all rights revert back to you and the contract terminates.

SUGGESTION: *Date of Publication clause = 1 year*

> Publication date should be about one year from the date of signing the contract.

Work with the Editor

An editor is not the enemy of a writer. Early in my writing career, while sitting in a bar in New York City, I met a writer who described editors as the "spawn of Satan." He was an unpublished writer, and I'm sure probably still is if he kept that attitude.

Editors are our friends, really. An editor wants the manuscript to be the best that it can possible be. She will point out things that a writer is too close to see. You may read a paragraph four times and never see that two words are reversed in order. That's because your mind knows what the sentences *should* say and corrects it in your head.

The editor's fresh set of eyes will catch those embarrassing things. She will offer advice on how to tighten up the plot and to make sure all the loose ends have been tied together.

SUGGESTION: *Allow time for an editor's comments sink in.*

> Every time, and I mean *every* time, I receive the editor's comments back on my latest book, my first reaction is:
>
> > *What? Is she crazy? That manuscript was pristine when I sent it to her. Now, it's covered with red ink.*
>
> I set the manuscript aside and have a beer or two. I wait a couple of days and mull around some of the editing suggestions. With an objective mind, I can see how the comments are quite astute and will make the manuscript better than I had ever thought possible.

Cover Art

Most writers have very little say in the cover art for their books. A book publisher's graphic designers know what works and why.

Look Professional

Readers really do judge a book by its cover. It had better look inviting, intriguing, and professional. A sloppy cover conveys a amateurish book.

Offer Your Suggestions

If, by the grace of your publisher, you are asked for ideas, keep it simple. You know the manuscript and themes better than anyone else at this point in production. Try to bring out a theme of the book or some image that the reader will be drawn to, but will also have an *ah-ha* moment when the reader looks at the cover after finishing the book.

Be eBook & Print Smart

On Internet websites and on eReader devices, a book's cover may be very small. Overly elaborate covers will look like a jumbled mess. Think what the cover will look like if it were the size of a postage stamp.

SUGGESTION: *Look at your cover from across the room.*

> One trick I learned from a book store owner was to view the book's cover mock-up from across the room.
>
> This is what a potential buyer would see walking into a store or approaching a book signing table or seeing the cover as a small image on a website.
>
> Is the cover easily recognizable? Can you read the title? Does the image standout or recede into the background? If you saw that cover again, would you remember it?

Marketing

This changes faster than technology. It is all about reaching readers and publicizing your book. Some basics that all writers should have:

- Website with your name (for example: www.GregLilly.com)

  This website should have:
  - Information about your book

  - Information about you

  - List of upcoming events

  - Media Kit that includes your bio, author picture, book cover image, book summary, blurbs from reviews, and contact information

- · Hyperlinks to buy the book at Amazon, Barnes & Noble, independent bookstores, and/or you

- Blog where you can share your thoughts and experiences on writing the book, the craft of writing, give-aways, special events, and promotions

- Facebook.com to connect with friends, relatives, and readers

- Goodreads.com to discuss books with other writers and readers

- Twitter.com to post thoughts about writing, books, and the subject of your expertise and book

- YouTube.com to post book trailers, if you use them (Book trailers are fun, but probably not worth the cost if you have to pay someone to do it for you.)

- Advertising on Facebook and Goodreads has not been successful for me because they tend to jack up the price per click so it is not cost effective

- Advertising in newspapers and magazines require a lot of money, so try press releases about events to get some publicity

Web & Social Media

Publicity — that's what the Internet and social media sites do for you. You can connect with readers and potential readers. They can give you feedback on the book. The more responsive you are, the better.

If someone takes the time to send you an e-mail, answer it. If someone replies to your blog, respond back.

Sites like Facebook, Goodreads, Twitter, and others can suck you in and be a huge time-waster. Interaction is good, but blowing the whole afternoon watching funny videos on YouTube doesn't get words on the paper.

Set a time limit on your social media interaction. Maybe check it at lunch or at the end of the day.

Author Events

Author events are the celebrations, happenings, functions, and affairs that all writers dream of holding. Adoring fans line up a few hours before the start time, giddy with excitement to hold a signed copy of your novel. Sigh. Sometimes my mom will treat me that way, but readers do not.

I have actually had a tumbleweed roll by my table will waiting for a visitor to stop to talk to me. It was Arizona and outside, so that's probably why, but the point is: An event can be lonely. It can also be exciting and packed with people. Predicting which way it turns out is difficult, but the safe bet is it will be a little of both.

An event's main purpose is publicity, not book sales. Sales are great, but few pay for the time and effort required for an event.

When you plan an event, send the information to the local papers, post signs, tweet on Twitter, post on Facebook and Goodreads, write about it on your blog, tell your mom and her friends, alert your critique group, shout it across the cubicles at work. Get the word out that there is an event with you and your book.

Even if only five people show, hundreds have been reminded that you are an author with a book available for purchase.

Event Survival Kit

Some items that I've found essential during events include:

- □ books — take enough that you can sell one to everyone you expect to show up at the event, but you'll probably only sell 10-20% of what you take; that's not bad!

- ☐ 3 or more Sharpies® — black, ultra fine point

- ☐ a box of Altoids® — fresh breath is good

- ☐ a pocket pack of Kleenex®

- ☐ travel size of your favorite pain reliever

- ☐ pocket mirror — in case you feel like something is stuck in your teeth, you don't have to run to the restroom to check

- ☐ pocket knife — not for defense, but in case you need to open a box or cut a rope to hang a banner or sign

- ☐ book holders — these are really sold as stands for decorative plates or dishes. I like the stands that fold up flat; they're much easier when traveling.

- ☐ bookmarks with your website printed on them

- ☐ postcards of your book cover with a space to sign — I like to sign these for the people who say they like eBooks. I'll sign the card and that's a reminder for them to buy the book for their eReader.

- ☐ "Signed Copy" stickers

- ☐ a dish of candy for the visitors to your table

- ☐ signage for the event:

  - ☐ table sign(s) to list the price, any charity you are donating to, a special significance for this event (like the book is set in this location)

  - ☐ banner to draw attention to your table (Make one that has your name and identifies you as an author — this generic banner can be used over and over at different events.)

- ☐ cash box and small bills — if you are collecting the money

I keep all of these things together in a cardboard box, ready to go, next to my boxes of extra books. The night before an event, I put this Event Survival Kit in the car along with any books I might need to supply.

Book Signings

Book stores are the worst place to have a book signing.

The customer is overwhelmed by the number of books, cards, coffee selections, stuffed toys, t-shirts, and people surrounding them.

Many will walk past your table, avoiding eye contact as if you were a used car salesman. Not to worry, you will sell a few books because you are around readers.

On the other hand, I have had great success in other venues. You may not have readers walking by, but you will be a surprise to the people and most will stop and talk to you. I have had book signings at coffee shops, tea shops, restaurants, outdoor festivals, and art galleries.

Anywhere people linger is a great place to engage someone in conversation about them and your book.

Wherever you set up your table, there are a few things to remember:

- Do not sit down — stand and greet each person that walks by the table

- Smile (I tend to hum the theme from *The Smurfs* because it makes me smile.)

- Have your *Pitch* ready to explain your book to a potential reader (See page 58 in the chapter on the query letter for creating the Pitch.)

- Say "hello" and offer the visitor some candy

- Ask them what types of stories they enjoy — whatever they say, try to hook it back to your book

- Even if they don't seem interested, offer them a bookmark to take along so they can remember you and the book

- Have fun because people can spot a grumpy author and they steer clear of those

Workshops

I love workshops. My background as a technical trainer comes out, and I like telling people what to do (in case you haven't noticed that yet).

Leading a workshop is fun. You will learn as much from the participants as they do from you. The process of getting a group of writers together and talking about the craft is exhilarating.

You demonstrate your expertise and promote your skills, hopefully selling a few books along the way.

Do workshops for the experience, not the book sales. Writers, aspiring or seasoned, don't have a lot of money to spend on other peoples' books, so don't expect a lot of sales.

Panel Discussions

Like a workshop, these are fun, but more so because you get to talk with other writers or experts in other fields.

Conferences usually have panel opportunities for attending writers. I always enjoy these and get to meet other writers.

I was once on a panel about diversity at the World Bank in Washington D.C. I was the only writer on this panel with documentary filmmakers, World Bank executives, and lobbyists. I was nervous, but once we started talking, I found I had a unique view and plenty to contribute.

Panel participation is great public relations. Get your name, image, brand, and books in the public eye. Even if you don't sell books, a panel discussion provides publicity.

Diversify Your Scope

Like any business, writers must diversify to survive. Fiction writing royalties cannot pay my bills, well not so far... Non-fiction pays much better.

Non-Fiction

I write and edit for a monthly magazine. The magazine focuses on profiles of local people. This is a steady stream of income since I write about six profiles and edit about nine others each month.

In addition to the magazine writing and editing, I freelance graphic design projects and create media releases.

Non-fiction writing powers businesses. Many times a company may try to get a sales person to write a press release or a brochure or an e-mail newsletter to save money. But, an article full of misspellings, grammatical errors, and confusing sentences does more harm to the company's reputation than saving a few dollars does good.

SUGGESTION: *Start your writing clips with volunteer pieces.*

> For new writers, examples of your writing help get you jobs. These examples are referred to as *clips*. That term comes from how we would clip out articles from magazines and newspapers.

> Start where you work today. Build your portfolio of clips by volunteering to write a press release or a brochure. Show your employer how well you can write, and management will love you. You will be more valuable for this extra skill.

> If your employer doesn't have that opportunity, volunteer at church or a non-profit or the neighborhood

association to write newsletters. Any published writing is considered a good clip.

Teach

Many writers with advanced degrees will teach college courses on different aspects of writing. This is a wonderful opportunity to help aspiring writers and to develop your own skills and creativity.

I envy the college environment and the immersion into a creative community. I've toyed with the idea of earning my Masters of Fine Arts in Creative Writing, but have not found the time to pursue it.

Conducting writing workshops is fun for me. Local libraries, writers groups, community colleges, and writers conferences will have opportunities for conducting workshops.

Publishing Industry

This is our industry. As writers we know how this works and doesn't work. Writers may work publishing jobs such as as literary agents, reviewers, bloggers, editors, ghost writers, marketers, distributors, publishers and printers.

I started Cherokee McGhee Publishing because of all the great writers and manuscripts that I saw getting passed over by the larger publishing houses. As a publisher, I'm using all the skills I've accumulated over the years to nurture and produce intriguing and entertaining books.

SUGGESTION: *Assess your skills & interests for opportunities.*

Writers are creative. Creative people are always in demand. Review what you enjoy doing and follow that path. Opportunity will present itself. Take a chance!

Have Fun

Publishing is a business. That doesn't mean it can't be fun. Put on your professional writer demeanor and act like you know what you're doing. That's what I do.

At the beginning of the Writer's Life, you take what jobs and assignments you can get. Some may be volunteering to produce your church's newsletter or taking photographs and penning an article for the community newspaper, but each piece you write becomes one more step on the journey.

Eventually, you'll get busy — really busy. The jobs you take will pay better. Businesses and readers will see your work and want more.

A small percentage of writers (like in any other field) become household names. Not all computer programmers become Bill Gates, and not all writers become Stephen King.

To succeed in the Writing Life, to live that dream, you have to love what you do. Then it isn't "work," it is "writing." There is no retirement from writing like there is retirement from work. Why would you retire from doing what you love?

Writers write. Let's get started on our next project!

Greg Lilly

Greg Lilly is the publisher at Cherokee McGhee, and he writes the Derek Mason Mystery series along with stand-alone novels and historical fiction. He is a former Arts & Culture Commissioner for the City of Sedona, Arizona and has served on a diversity panel at The World Bank in Washington D.C.

When not writing novels, Greg is a seminar presenter on writing and publishing topics such as pace, setting, effective query letters, overcoming writer's block, and short story writing, and is a facilitator of Julia Cameron's creativity workshop *The Artist's Way*.

He is a freelance writer and graphic artist whose work has appeared in *Southwest Art*, *Cowboys & Indians*, *Sedona Monthly*, *American Art Collector*, and *Western Art & Architecture* magazines.

Greg is the former managing editor of *Sedona Home & Garden* magazine and is the current editor for Williamsburg's *Next Door Neighbors* magazine.

He founded Cherokee McGhee publishing in 2007 after careers in information technology, magazine publishing, marketing, and as a published novelist. The first novel released by Cherokee McGhee was Greg's third book, the historical novel *Under a Copper Moon*. Using his author experiences with publishers and agents, he honed the publishing processes, resources, and schedules while employing new technology to create a distributed and efficient business model.

Today, Cherokee McGhee's catalog includes two imprints and twelve novels with two more books slated for release in the coming year.

He writes and lives in the Tidewater area of Virginia.

www.GregLilly.com

www.CherokeeMcGhee.com

CPSIA information can be obtained at www.ICGtesting.com
Printed in the USA
LVOW08s1540230813

349370LV00009B/776/P